STOCK-PICKING REVISITED

Don Johnston

COPYRIGHT

ISBN: 978-0-578-98789-7

Stock-Picking Revisited describes a method of developing a stock portfolio that will outperform the Dow Jones Industrial Average (DJIA).

DEDICATION AND SPECIAL THANKS

This book is dedicated to my family and friends, especially my friends at Sugar Land Baptist Church.

My special thanks to Janice Stewart for her proofreading and editing help and also for suggesting the title.

OTHER BOOKS BY DON JOHNSTON

The Dar Lumbre Chronicles

"A clever extrapolation of today's sociopolitical pathologies in the next century."

"...ingenious narrative..."   – *Kirkus Reviews*

"Truly a sci-fi book, *The Dar Lumbre Chronicles* was very entertaining."

– *CityBook Review*

The Alamogordo Connection

"First contact is an intriguing hook, made more effective through believable details of carrying out scientific research and rainforest trekking, bolstered by Johnston's background in biology, chemistry, and jungle survival."

– *Kirkus Reviews*

TABLE OF CONTENTS

Prologue

Who is the greatest stock-picker of all time, Peter Lynch or Warren Buffett?

Let's chase a rabbit for a minute—it will help answer this question.

Among retired MLB starting pitchers, who is the best strikeout pitcher of all time? Is it Randy Johnson or Nolan Ryan? Ryan pitched for 27 years and holds the strikeout record (5714 strikeouts); he struck out 9.55 batters per 9 innings pitched. Johnson pitched for 22 years and struck out 4875 batters for an average of 10.61 batters per 9 innings pitched; during his heyday, he was the most feared pitcher in baseball. So I give the nod to Johnson as the best strikeout pitcher of all times, although he didn't have the longevity that Ryan had.

Now, back to Mr. Lynch and Mr. Buffett.

Warren Buffett, one of the most successful businessmen in the world, has been Chairman of Berkshire Hathaway since 1970 and has made over $100 billion through his investments. In addition, he is well known as a philanthropist; his accomplishments are truly amazing, and he is still going strong at 90 years old. We could learn a lot from him.

Peter Lynch was the manager of the Fidelity Magellan Fund from 1977 until 1990. During his tenure, Magellan was the top-ranked general equity fund in the world. An investment of $1000 in Magellan in 1977 was worth $28,000 in 1990. This is 29% growth, compounded annually for 13 years. I don't believe anyone will ever beat Lynch; he is the GOAT (*G*reatest *Of A*ll *T*ime).

So, although Randy Johnson and Peter Lynch were the best at what they did, Nolan Ryan and Warren Buffett accomplished more because they stayed at it longer. This brings me to a major point.

Time in the market is more important than timing the market.

Remember, the tortoise beat the hare. Start investing immediately. Develop a plan and stick with it. Read on and I'll tell you how to pick stocks like a pro, maybe better.

Happy investing!

Chapter 1
Getting Started

I'm not an MBA, CPA, financial advisor, management consultant, stockbroker, or any other kind of recognized financial expert with initials after my name. With one course in bookkeeping in high school and *An Introduction to Accounting* in college, the only letters that I can affix to my name are BA, and that degree is in chemistry and biology, the fields in which I have worked for about 60 years.

Still, after more than 40 years of managing my own portfolios, I've evolved into a rather good stock-picker and would like to pass along some of my stock-picking techniques to others who are actively involved in managing their own investments. The method presented herein can be used for picking stocks, mutual funds, and exchange traded funds (ETF's), but does not address the purchase of bonds, bond funds, annuities, precious metals, crypto currencies, commodities, options, CD's, etc. These securities are an important part of many portfolios, but I claim no expertise in any of them.

In spite of the disclaimer stated in the first paragraph above, over the past 15+ years, a number of people have asked me which stocks I like best. Generally, when this happens, I give them a short list of my favorite stocks from my portfolio and let it go at that. A few people actually bought some of the stocks, but most didn't. One notable exception–in 2011, a good friend asked me the *favorite-stock* question. I answered, "Apple," and he put a substantial amount of money into the stock. Now, he is an even better friend! By the way, I can prove this story. Other than discussions with my family, most of my stock-market conversations have been with friends about my age.

Well, maybe not quite *that* old! However, some young people have asked for my advice recently. Therefore, I'll start with some advice suitable for those in their teens or early twenties and go on to advice that is suitable for everyone.

The first thing anyone should do after getting a job is set up a Roth IRA. Funds contributed to the Roth IRA are not tax deductible going in, but are tax deductible coming out. Currently (2021), if your adjusted gross income is over $125,000 (single) or $198,000 (married, filing jointly), you cannot have a Roth IRA.

If you don't qualify for a Roth IRA, you can still open a regular IRA. Capital appreciation, dividends, and interest accumulate tax free until drawn out, and the contribution itself is deductible on your 1040 form unless you are participating in a company-sponsored retirement plan (Keogh, SEP/IRA, 401(k), etc.). Regular IRA's have strict rules regarding withdrawal of funds, so if this is your choice, you should review the rules before opening one. In any case, if you have a job, you should have an IRA or a Roth IRA. There's no better way to start saving.

My advice to any teenager or young adult (or anyone else who hasn't done so) is to open an account with an online bank/brokerage firm where you can **(1)** set up a Roth IRA or a regular IRA, **(2)** invest regularly in securities, **(3)** write checks, and **(4)** get a debit or credit card.

If you don't have an account as described above, open one now. Do it even if you can only save a few dollars from a summer job or part time work. **Begin saving regularly, no matter how small the amount**. Eventually you will save enough to begin buying securities.

If you are in your teens, twenties, thirties, and forties, time is your ally. You can ride out a bear market because you won't need the money to retire any time soon.

My first rule of investing is this: invest regularly in good stocks, ETF's, and mutual fund and hold them forever (forever is a relative term in the stock market). Don't spend a lot of time trying to time the market–the worst mistake most people make is jumping in and out of stocks as the market fluctuates. In other words, I'm recommending a long-term approach. **I don't have a get-rich-quick plan!**

It should be obvious from the above discussion that I've concentrated primarily on purchasing shares of established companies to build a portfolio. If you do this, you can expect steady growth over the years. Nearly all stock-pickers dream of picking the next big thing, maybe a *ten-bagger*. My advice–forget that idea for a few years, at least until you have enough extra cash in your account to risk a small amount on speculative stocks.

When you get ready to try your hand at picking stocks, choose several stocks for your Roth IRA (or regular IRA) and plan on holding them for a long, long time. Start with five or more stocks and add others as you can.

Full Disclosure Statement–although I've discouraged speculation in the above discourse, I do give it a shot once in a while; however, I don't speculate in my investment portfolio, which I call *Don's Best Picks*. A few years ago, I opened a separate account–a much smaller one that I call my *Casino Account*. If I get the urge to buy stock in an emerging company, I buy a small amount in this account. That way, it doesn't affect my investment portfolio.

Don't bet on the *next big thing* unless you do it with money you can afford to lose!

The rest of the information in this book is designed to show you how to select good securities (primarily stocks and exchange traded funds). The method that I will show you in Chapter 10 is simple, yet it is one of the best stock-picking techniques I've ever seen. I can't find anyone else touting this method, so I'm claiming it as my own invention.

Six ways to invest are shown below (I've tinkered with all of them with varying degrees of success):

1. Market timing
2. Bottom fishing (or contrarian approach)
3. Momentum investing
4. Growth-stock investing
5. Value investing (or fundamental approach)
6. Dividend investing

My method of picking stocks does not match any of the above methods exactly, but some familiarity with each of them should help you understand my method when we get to it.

We'll take a look at each of these methods, beginning with *Market Timing* in Chapter 2.

Chapter 2
Market Timing

The market doesn't go straight up; uptrends and downtrends are a normal part of investing. When the market goes up, most stocks go up as well, and when the market declines, most stocks follow suit. Investors should learn to live with these fluctuations.

Knowing that a downturn is inevitable at some point, many investors keep a high percentage of their portfolios in cash with the idea of jumping into the fray at the next pullback, correction, or bear market. Since it's impossible to time the market, no one can tell how far a downturn will go until it ends. Even so, market-timers are determined to try, and many rely on various indicators, particularly charts. Of special interest, of course, are chart patterns that signal a reversal in the market's direction.

In order to categorize market fluctuations in useful terms, most analysts group downturns into the following three categories:

1. Pullbacks: downturns less than 10% from an all-time high.

2. Corrections: downturns more than 10%, but less than 20%, from an all-time high.

3. Bear markets: downturns 20% or more from an all-time high.

With differing opinions among professional analysts as to whether some sharp downturns in the past were corrections or actually bear markets, there have been about 21 corrections/bear markets since 1920 and enough substantial pullbacks to average one significant downturn approximately every 4 years. Various sources report that the average bear market lasts a little over a year. Consequently, investors have to accept one indisputable fact: **The market will take a sharp downturn sometime in the future** (it could start today).

Can analysts predict the market's direction?

Not very well. In *Winning on Wall Street,* Martin Zweig described a *Barron's* ad "market indicator." Simply put, if there were as many as 20 bullish ads in *Barron's,* the market was likely headed for a downturn. If there were seven or fewer bullish ads and any bearish ads, the market was probably about to move upward in the near future. In other words, the consensus of opinion among professionals served as a *reverse indicator.* They certainly weren't any help to those wanting to time the market.

At any rate, the question for market-timers is this: **what stocks should you buy when the market pulls back?**

The internet is overloaded with articles (*advertisements,* actually) written by financial advisors on this subject. Headlines pop up constantly on every financial webpage on the internet. Below are some recent ones:

"A Stock Market Crash Is On The way; Three stocks to Buy When It Happens"

"High-Dividend Stocks for the Next Pullback"

"The Best Big-Cap Stocks to Buy On a Pullback"

"Earn 35% on This High-dividend stock"

"Worried About the Delta Variant? 5 Stocks to Insulate You From a COVID Market Crash"

"3 EV Stocks That Can Survive the Next Market Crash"

The first headline above (July 23, 2021) was posted by a financial advisory company that seems ubiquitous on the internet. They advocated buying three high dividend stocks during the next correction (and subscribing to their service, of course). The stocks were JNJ, NLY, and DUK (Johnson & Johnson, Annaly Capital Management, and Duke Energy). While market performance during and after the COVID-19 crash in the spring of 2020 is no guarantee of what will happen during the next crash, it is probably a reasonable indicator. At any rate, it is a worthwhile study, so I decided to evaluate this recommendation to see if the advice seemed worth considering.

A preliminary analysis showed that NLY had outperformed JNJ and DUK from the 2020 crash until July 23, 2021, so it was the best pick from the article/advertisement, and I used it for the study as follows.

First, using the stock charts from Yahoo Finance's web page, I found the absolutely lowest price for which NLY could have been bought during the 2020 bear market and "invested" $10,000 at that price. Next, I "sold" it at the highest price it reached on July 23, 2021. The dividend was listed as 10.49% on that date, so I back calculated the dividend to the lowest possible purchase price and came up with a calculated dividend of 19.55% when purchased. I accumulated dividends for 16 months (March 2020 through July 2021).

Figures Used for Calculations

NLY price at its low (4-3-2020):   4.56
NLY price at its high on 7-23-2021:   8.50
Dividend on 7-23-2021:   10.49%
Calculated dividend on 4-3-2020:   19.55%

Results for NLY:

       $8,640 capital gains
        2,606 dividend gains
     $11,246 total gains

Using the exact same methodology, the following results were obtained by analyzing some of my favorite securities "bought" during this time period. My selections were Apple, First Dow Internet Fund, Applied Materials, and Global Lithium Exchange Traded Fund.

AAPL: $16,909 total gains
FDN: $13,823 total gains
AMAT: $28,048 total gains
LIT: $35,543 total gains

As you can see, my selections trounced the experts' advice by a wide margin during the last bear market, and I feel certain they would do so during the next one. Interestingly, nearly all of the *market-crash advice* involves buying high-dividend stocks. I've never understood why this is the most often-recommended approach. High-performing stocks (which I will show you how to select) will beat high-dividend stocks. Besides, anyone can make a profit on nearly any stock by buying it at its absolute lowest price (who can do that?). This recommendation was worthless.

Let me set the record straight—I did not buy the four stocks listed above during the COVID crash. I owned APPL and FDN before the crash and bought AMAT and LIT after the crash. They all went through the crash in the spring of 2020 and have soared since (especially AMAT and LIT), while NLY has yet to reach its pre-COVID level as I write this (July 31, 2021). DUK has just passed its pre-COVID level, and JNJ is doing well.

The second headline above led to an article touting four high-dividend stocks to buy at the next pullback: NLY, EPD, MBT, and AGNC. I was 100% certain that my selections would beat these four stocks (they'd already beaten NLY), so I didn't perform the calculations on the remaining three. However, if you want to do it yourself, just follow the procedure outlined above. You'll find that my selections will outperform the "experts" again. In fact, the next time the market crashes, I'll seriously consider *betting the farm* on LIT and AMAT.

The above statements could lead you to believe that I'm opposed to buying dividend stocks (or high-dividend stocks). That's absolutely not the case. I've owned some of these stocks for a long time and plan to keep them. What I oppose is bogus claims that "experts" circulate about buying stocks, specifically, that the high-dividend stocks will outperform all other securities during a crash. That is simply not the case. They won't beat APPL, AMAT, LIT or hundreds of other stocks.

Regarding dividend stocks, one of my most thorough stock market studies was performed on the list known as the Dividend Aristocrats (DA's). Simply put, DA's are stocks (65 stocks in 2021) that have increased dividends annually for at least 25 years. I learned a lot from this study.

The DA list contains some great stocks, some good stocks, and some dogs. I'll show you how to tell the difference.

What I want you to take away from Chapter 2 is this: **stocks which are doing the best before a crash will likely do the best after a crash.** There is no advantage in having one group of stocks to invest in while things are *normal*, and another group to invest in during a crash.

Forget about timing the market. Buy good stocks and hold them forever.

Let's move on to Chapter 3, *Bottom Fishing*.

Chapter 3
Bottom Fishing

Bottom-fishing is such a good metaphor that I'll probably overwork it a little in this chapter.

What some people call bottom fishing, professional money managers generally refer to as the contrarian approach. It's an investment strategy somewhat like market timing. However, instead of waiting for the whole market to pull back, the bottom-fisher waits for certain stocks (usually from a *wish list*) to pull back and then buys the stock. Currently (August 2021), bottom-fishers are buying the airlines and cruise lines, which tanked during the COVID-19 market crash. This is a bold move which could result in a very nice profit, but carries the possibility of a substantial loss as well (what stock doesn't?).

Bottom fishing embraces the old concept, buy low and sell high. Before buying a stock, the bottom-fisher must have a reason to believe that it is undervalued and will turn upward in the future, hopefully the not-too-distant future. However, in some cases the wait is so long that the investor becomes impatient and sells too soon, often just before the stock turns upward (I've done this several times myself). Moreover, there is always a risk that the stock will continue sinking until the bottom-fisher finds his recent purchase "under water." Consequently, it's best to have a price in mind when it's time to "abandon ship." This can easily be done by putting a *stop loss* under the stock when purchased, so it will sell automatically if the price drops to a certain point.

One could argue that bottom fishing is a form of *value investing*, i.e., by determining the real value of a company's stock through careful analysis of its P&L Statement and future prospects, the investor decides that the stock has more upside potential than downside risk. As I understand it, based on this type of analysis, a true value-investor might occasionally buy a stock near its all-time high. A devout bottom-fisher would never do such a thing!

Many years ago, I tried my hand at bottom fishing. It was difficult to work up a good prospect list and set parameters for buying and selling the stocks. Bottom-fishing advisors vary all over the board in their recommendations. Some of them advise buying a stock when it approaches its 52-week low, which is easy to track. Others rely on charts with moving averages and other complex chart patterns that rival Einstein's Theory of Relativity.

After a lot of trouble trying to figure out how to get started, I gave up on the idea of going it alone and subscribed to a bottom-fishing newsletter. The newsletter's approach was very simple. It presented a list of stocks to buy and also advised the subscriber when it was time to sell. The process worked reasonably well, and the newsletter showed up on a list as one of the best newsletters of the year (this was so long ago that I've forgotten the exact name of the newsletter and the year that I subscribed to it).

Still, something was missing. I wanted to do everything by myself, rather than having someone telling me every move to make.

About 1995, I stumbled upon a book by Michael O'Higgins. This book, *Beating the Dow* (published in 1990, revised in 2000), describes a concept called "Dogs of the Dow." This investment strategy is a form of bottom fishing, although Mr. O'Higgins refers to himself as a contrarian.

The Dogs concept is based on selecting the highest dividend-paying stocks in the DJIA. This approach seems to meet the requirements of both the bottom-fisher and the dividend-investor. Moreover, it's a *Gone Fishing* portfolio because adjustments are needed only once a year.

The Dogs of the Dow stock-picking process is described below:

Late in December, preferably the last trading day, pull up a list of the Dow Thirty (DJIA) and select the 10 stocks that are paying the highest dividends. Invest an equal amount in each of the stocks and forget about them for a year. When the following December rolls around, adjust the portfolio as required, i.e., sell all stocks that are no longer on the "Dogs" list and add any new ones that appear. This process zeroes in on stocks which have dropped during the year but continue to pay the same dividend, thus the dividend "rises" as a percentage of the stock's price.

If an investor goes all in on this stock-picking method, the 30 stocks in the DJIA become the entire stock universe. Moreover, portfolios assembled by the Dogs method would consist of only 10 stocks.

The process can be further streamlined by selecting only the "Small Dogs," that is, the five stocks with the lowest price. The Dogs of the Dow website reports that the Small Dog approach has been the best for the last five years or so.

Does this stock-picking strategy really work?

The short answer is, "Yes, it works very well." However, there are a couple of caveats that we need to discuss after looking over the current list shown below.

Current Dogs of the Dow (selected 12-31-2020):

Ticker Symbol	Company	Price	Dividend, %
CVX	Chevron	84.45	6.11
IBM	IBM	125.88	5.18
DOW	Dow Chemical	55.50	5.05
WBA	Walgreens	39.88	4.69
VZ	Verizon	58.75	4.27
MMM	3M	174.79	3.36
CSCO	Cisco	44.39	3.24
MRK	Merck	81.80	3.18
AMGN	Amgen	229.92	3.06
KO	Coca-Cola	54.84	2.99

The above information is from **www.dogsofthedow.com**.

The Small Dogs on the 2020 list are DOW, WBA, VZ, CISCO, and KO. I did a quick check by setting up a model portfolio containing only these five stocks. Incredibly (yes, I was surprised), this portfolio did beat the DJIA slightly during the first six months of 2021.

In addition to the above 2020 list, let's examine the lists for 2019, 2018, 2017, and 2016. You can easily go to the above website and check them for yourself, so I didn't work up a complete list for each year.

The first thing that sticks out like a sore thumb is that IBM, VZ, CVX, CSCO, and MRK have been on the Dogs list for five years running (maybe more; that's as far back as I went). They've been bottom dwellers for a long time, which means they've experienced very little capital appreciation. This also points out one reason why the Small Dog approach has been the most effective for the last five years.

It eliminates two lagging Big Dogs, IBM and CVX. I'm not saying that these two stocks will never go up, but they're certainly taking their time about it. KO is not much better; it has been on the Dogs list four of the last five years.

Over the past five years, the following stocks were on the Dogs list but have rotated off: Exxon, JP Morgan, Proctor & Gamble, Pfizer, General Electric, Boeing, Caterpillar, and Walmart. Obviously, stocks rotate off the list because their prices go up.

Anyone using the Dogs of the Dow method of picking stocks for the last five years would have bought Walmart and Caterpillar in 2016, and JP Morgan in 2019. The excellent performance of these three stocks would have made up for General Electric and Exxon's flatline performance. The remaining stocks in the rotation performed reasonably well.

Now, let's look at a couple of problem areas.

One major short-coming in the Dog process is this–if you were following the recommended buy/sell procedure exactly as described, you would have already sold CAT, WMT, and JPM. The truth is, these are good stocks to buy and hold. I've owned all three of them in the past, but don't own any of them currently, which points out that I made a blunder somewhere along the way.

Another shortcoming in this method of investing is that, if your portfolio is not in an IRA or similarly protected retirement fund, profit is taxable in the year that you sell stocks which are showing a profit. My largest portfolio is not in an IRA, so I try to accumulate *unrealized gains,* rather than take profit and pay taxes. This makes me a *buy and hold* investor as much as possible.

Below is an example showing one reason why the Small Dogs perform better than the entire 10-stock Dog portfolio.

As Coach Lou Holtz says, "This is not something that I read in a book; it's something that happened to me."

In early January of 2016, I bought some Chevron stock and held it until January of 2021. Although I wasn't thinking of the Dogs of the Dow at the time, the buy/sell dates were so close to the recommended Dog procedure that I later came to think of it as a Dog purchase (actually, it was!). After selling the stock, I gave it a thorough analysis by comparing it to DIA on the basis of growth and dividends earned for the five-year holding period. DIA is an ETF (exchange traded fund) that tracks the performance of the Dow 30. For several years, DIA has been my benchmark for evaluating other potential purchases.

To perform the analysis, I "invested" $10,000 in CHV and DIA at the opening bell on January 4, 2016, and "sold" it on January 4, 2021, at the opening bell. Next, I calculated the dividends on each security for five years and added that figure to the value of the security. I didn't compound the dividends because I accumulate them as cash, rather than reinvesting them in the stocks that paid them. For those who would like to see the difference, the compounded dividends are shown in parenthesis in the study below.

Prices and Dividends Used for This Study

Ticker Symbol	Dividend	Price 1-4-2016	Price 1-4-2021
DIA	1.68%	163.24	306.59
CHV	4.70%	90.00	93.00

Results for DIA

Gain from dividends	$ 840	($ 854)
Gain due to increase in price	8,782	
Total gain	9,622	
Total value after 5 years	$ 19,622	

Results for CHV

Gain from dividends	$ 2,350	($ 2,643)
Gain due to increase in price	333	
Total gain	2,683	
Total value after 5 years	$ 12,683	

Conclusion: I made a mistake when I bought CHV. It had almost no capital appreciation in five years.

This chapter illustrates that bottom fishing is a valid way to invest, especially if done according to The Dogs of the Dow procedures. Moreover, it shows one reason why Small Dogs are likely to perform better than the entire Dog portfolio.

If I hadn't discovered a better way to pick stocks, I would have no qualms about using the Small Dogs approach; however, I would modify the procedure and keep stocks like Caterpillar, Walmart, and JP Morgan.

That's enough bottom fishing. Let's move on to *Momentum Investing* in Chapter 4.

Chapter 4
Momentum Investing

Momentum investing is a strategy that attempts to capitalize on the continuation of existing trends in the market. This approach embraces the concept, *The trend is your friend.* The theory holds that it's possible to profit by staying with a trend until its conclusion, no matter how long that may be. For example, momentum investors that entered the stock market in 2009 enjoyed an uptrend that lasted about nine years.

I've only tried this approach a couple of times and know just enough about it to be dangerous, but since it's almost the exact opposite of bottom fishing, let's take a brief look at it.

Momentum-investors purchase securities that are showing an upward price trend. In addition, they often short sell securities that are showing a downward trend. The theory behind this type of investing is that, once a trend is well established, it is likely to continue for some time. There is very little consensus among economists, financial advisors money managers, or anybody else regarding the validity of this theory. In my opinion, investors bear a tremendous risk when implementing this strategy; however, they sometimes reap significant rewards.

Many people consider Richard Driehaus to be the originator of momentum investing. Mr. Driehaus (who died March 9, 2021) was an American fund manager, investor, and philanthropist. He took exception to the old stock market adage, *Buy low and sell high,* and is quoted as saying, "Far more money is made by buying high and selling at even higher prices."

The rise of the FANG stocks (Facebook, Apple, Amazon, Netflix, and Google) provides some evidence to support Driehaus' concept. These five stocks have provided many opportunities for momentum investors to put this system into practice and make a tremendous profit. Of course, these stocks also did extremely well for the *buy-and-hold* investor. It took no special skills to make a profit off the FANG stocks. Everyone who has held these stocks for a long period of time has been rewarded handsomely, and I think they still have plenty of room to grow.

Tools Used in Momentum Trading

Since momentum-investors spend a tremendous amount of time trying to determine the direction and strength of market trends, knowledge of key technical indicators is crucial. While trying to learn enough about momentum indicators to write this brief chapter, I came across the following list of commonly used indicators in this type of investing:

1. Trend Lines
2. Moving Averages
3. Stochastic Oscillators
4. Average Directional Indexes

Does this sound incredibly complicated to you? It does to me. In addition, I found a couple of other indicators that are somewhat related to the above four but didn't see any value in listing them.

I could explain the first two, but the last two are beyond the scope of this book and beyond my comprehension as well.

Read the following story and we'll leave it at that.

Ballet Dancing, Momentum Investing, and Day-Trading

In the late 1980's or early 1990's I was watching a financial program on TV. The conversation was about using different investment methods, and one of the participants was discussing momentum investing. Specifically, he said that the famous Russian ballet dancer, Rudolph Nureyev, was a momentum investor and only bought stocks when they reached a new high. Since I know absolutely nothing about dancing ballet and little more about momentum investing, this story doesn't fit my narrative very well, but it was so unusual that it stuck in my mind.

Momentum investing blossomed in the early 2000's with the rise of the dot-com stocks. This era also spawned Day-Trading companies that maintained a bank of computers for rent. Many of the day-traders (I don't think they were really *investors*) were trying to catch a stock with short-term momentum, generally just one day. Nearly all of the traders lost money, and several lawsuits resulted. In one lawsuit, a day-trading company was forced to reveal its customer list. As I recall, it had 62 customers and 61 of them had lost money.

So much for becoming a day-trading momentum-investor (or a ballet dancer!).

Let's forget about this investment method and move on to *Growth-Stock Investing* in Chapter 5.

Chapter 5
Growth-Stock Investing

Growth-stock investors search for companies that are expected to enjoy a surge in growth and profit. Most of the time, the prospects are emerging companies; sometimes the companies are also in an emerging industry, but not always. Purchasing stocks in young companies carries a higher risk than most other forms of investing, as evidenced in the dot-com bubble that surged from 1995 to March 2000, after which it burst. This bubble was caused by excessive speculation in internet-related companies that had no possibility of attaining the profits anticipated. No matter how great the possibilities of making a profit appear for a company, sooner or later, that possibility has to turn into reality or the company's stock will crash.

Unlike the frenzied dot-com investors, or the momentum-investors discussed in the last chapter, **true growth stock investors are value investors**, constantly analyzing every aspect of the company's business, including earnings (current and projected), new products and services, pricing, competition, institutional interest, market direction, and much more. This type of analysis would be a tremendous amount of work for the individual investor, so much, in fact, that most people probably should not attempt it without professional help.

The greatest growth-stock investor of all times is Peter Lynch, whom I mentioned in the Prologue. Mr. Lynch retired from the Magellan Fund in 1990, so he didn't face the dot-com incident as Magellan's manager. However, after reading his books, *One Up on Wall Street* and *Beating the Street*, I'm convinced that he was far too smart to fall into such a trap.

In *Beating the Street,* Lynch states that it was a small number of major successes ("10-baggers," he calls them) which were the reason behind his remarkable success. He states that it takes only one or two such companies in a decade to turn an average portfolio into a major winner.

Actually, Mr. Lynch was far too modest; he certainly found more than one or two major winners per decade.

Below are a few of the emerging companies that he discovered before they were household names:

Walmart
Home Depot (Mr. Lynch said he sold HD too soon)
Hanes
Taco Bell
Cracker Barrel (a "50-bagger")
Nike
Reebok
Dunkin' Donuts
Kentucky Fried Chicken

Pretty impressive list, wouldn't you say?

I check my performance against Warren Buffett from time to time; however, Peter Lynch set the bar too high (29% growth compounded annually for 13 Years). The only growth-stock investing that I've tried was in my *Casino Account*. In the paragraph below, I tell you enough about the experience to prove that there are better ways to invest.

Since I didn't have the inclination to perform the analysis necessary to determine a young company's possibilities, I decided to base my analysis on chemistry and biology (Why not? My degree is in these subjects!).

I put together a list of small biotech and drug companies and went to each company's website to see if what they were doing was feasible from the chemistry/biology standpoint, and if the products seemed to be marketable. This worked pretty well for several years, and I actually snagged a "5-bagger" (AMRN). However, when the COVID-19 market crash occurred, most of these small companies dropped like lead balloons.

Currently, I'm trying a different approach in my *Casino Account!*

Okay, I'm not a good growth-stock investor; however, I mentioned it because it's regularly discussed in books on the subject of investing.

Let's move on to *Value Investing* in Chapter 6.

Chapter 6
Value Investing

Warren Buffett is king of the hill when it comes to value investing. He has done it successfully for a long time and many people consider him to be the patriarch of this type of investing. Mr. Buffett believes that investors should buy stocks in companies with solid fundamentals, strong earnings power, and long-term growth potential. These may sound like fairly simple concepts, but finding them is not always easy to do.

Value investing techniques vary from person to person; however, some general principles shared by all are listed below.

Buy Companies in Good Business Sectors

Basically, this means the value-investor should ignore the current market hype and study the fundamentals of the company being considered. Searching for companies in good business sectors with shares at a reasonable price takes considerable time and effort, but there's no other way to be a successful value-investor.

Invest in Companies You Understand

Critics of value investing are quick to point out this limitation. Since nobody is able to understand every kind of business, many good companies are never considered. Warren Buffett restricts his investments to companies that he can easily analyze. As a result, he did not suffer significant loss during the dot-com meltdown in the early 2000's, while many investors got wiped out.

Simple businesses have another distinct advantage; it is much harder for incompetent management to damage the company, a concept that leads to the next point.

Find Well-Managed Companies

Good management adds value beyond that seen on the balance sheet. Conversely, in a short period of time, poor management can destroy solid financials. Mr. Buffett advises investors to look for three things in management: intelligence, integrity, and energy.

You can get an idea of management's ability by examining several years of financial records. Did they deliver what they promised? If not, did they take responsibility for their shortcomings, or try to sweep them under the rug? Moreover, good managers look beyond the current price of the company's stock and focus on growing the business, thus creating long-term shareholder value.

Don't Over-Diversify

In this area, value investing runs contrary to conventional wisdom. Sometimes, there are long periods of time when a value investor cannot find a stock that is not overpriced. Toward the end of a long bull market, everything is too expensive, even the dogs. A value-investor may wait it out until a correction occurs.

Time, a valuable commodity, is lost while waiting to invest, so when you do find an undervalued stock, buy as much as you can afford. This will result in a portfolio that some would say is not well balanced by normal standards; however, value-investors are content to hold fewer stocks. Mr. Buffett often keeps more than 90% of his investment in

10 stocks or less.

Your Best-Performing Stock Is Your Guide To Future Purchases

Any time you have additional capital to invest, your aim should not necessarily be to become more diversified, but to find an investment better than the ones you already own. If your buying opportunities don't beat the stocks you already own, you may as well buy more of what you have. That is how Mr. Buffett ends up with so much capital invested in a few stocks, and it works for him.

Ignore the Market Most of the Time

The direction of the market matters primarily when you buy or sell a position. The rest of the time, you should ignore it for the most part. Generally you should keep holding a stock as long as its fundamentals remain strong. There will be times when you're holding an investment with a large unrealized gain that you could sell at a profit, and other times when you're holding an unrealized loss. This is the nature of market volatility. To be a successful investor, you have to learn how to live with it.

Be just as slow to sell as to buy. When you sell a security at a profit, you expose yourself to tax liability and may need to sell another stock with a loss to balance it out. The longer you can avoid taking a capital gain, the better off you'll be in the long run.

Holding Cash in Reserve vs Investing It

Sometimes it may seem that no attractively priced stocks are available to the value-investor.

Warren Buffett is known for keeping a large cash reserve in Berkshire Hathaway's holdings. Recently, I read that this balance had reached $109 billion.

That's a lot of idle money!

Two men mentioned in the Prologue, Warren Buffett and Peter Lynch are my investment heroes. How do these two men compare when it comes to their view of holding cash? They are completely different. While manager of the Fidelity Magellan Fund, Peter Lynch was not known for keeping a large cash reserve; he kept nearly all of it invested.

Which man was the most successful?

During Lynch's tenure at Magellan, the fund grew at a compounded annual rate of 29%. Berkshire Hathaway didn't do that well. **The conclusion should be obvious– funds kept in the market constantly will outperform cash being held outside the market while waiting for a downturn,**

Next, we'll look at *Dividend Investing* in Chapter 7.

Chapter 7
Dividend Investing

Dividend investors focus on developing a portfolio of high-dividend stocks, exchange traded funds and mutual funds

When people begin to consider retirement, they sometimes become oriented toward more stable income such as bonds which pay interest, or other securities which pay dividends. Historically, bonds have never kept pace with stocks, mutual funds, and ETF's. The reason is obvious. When companies grow more profitable, they often share the wealth with their investors in the form of dividend increases; however, in the history of the world, no company has rewarded its bondholders with an increase in interest rates on bonds they are holding. So let's skip bonds and concentrate on securities that pay dividends.

Publicly traded companies have three options when they generate a profit: **(1)** utilize the profit to grow the company, **(2)** purchase company stock to increase the value of the outstanding shares, or **(3)** pay dividends to their shareholders. In addition to being important to investors, dividends are important to the companies that pay them, especially those companies whose dividends are high enough to attract the attention of potential investors.

When looking for dividend stocks, investors should look, not only at the dividend, but also at the history of dividend growth. In addition, it's important to make sure that the valuation of the stock is in line with other companies in the same industry. As with any other investment, do enough research on the company to make sure that you're not about to invest in an overvalued stock.

Key point in this chapter: good dividend stocks must have the potential to achieve worthwhile capital appreciation. Sometimes dividend-investors buy stocks based solely on the size of the dividend without paying much attention to the company's future growth prospects. This is a big mistake. As you read on, I will identify some popular high-dividend stocks which exhibit perpetually-lagging growth. In addition, I'll show you how to identify those dividend stocks which exhibit excellent capital appreciation.

Some Popular Dividend Securities

Utility Companies build infrastructure to provide water, electricity, gas, and other necessities. These companies pay some of the highest dividends in the stock market today.

The Energy Sector is known for paying high dividends. These stocks fluctuate with the price of oil and gas; moreover, this sector has been under pressure in recent years due to environmental concerns.

Specialized High-Dividend Securities that are popular today include the following:

REIT's - A *real estate investment trust* is a company that owns, operates, or finances income-producing properties.

CEF's - A *closed end fund* manages a portfolio of securities. These funds are closed in the sense that capital does not regularly flow in and out of them when investors buy and sell shares. Instead, shares are traded on an exchange with investors as buyers or sellers.

BDC's - A *business development company* invests in small and medium sized companies, sometimes concentrating on those that are having problems.

MLP's - A *master limited partnership* is a business venture existing as a publicly traded limited partnership.

Shares of these specialized securities trade just like any other stock. We will look more closely at several of them in Chapter 14.

Lists of Dividend Stocks have been around for years. One of the first was Moody's *Handbook of Dividend Achievers* (1992 edition), which listed 134 stocks with 20+ years of dividend increases and 362 stocks with a 10-year record. At the time this handbook was published, I wasn't focusing on dividends and didn't know such a list existed.

Around 10 years ago, I discovered the **Dividend Aristocrats (DA's).** This is a list of companies in the S&P 500 that have increased their dividends for 25 consecutive years or more. Several variations of the Dividend Aristocrat list have been composed, including lists based on the S&P 400 and the S&P 1500. These lists are similar. The list of Dividend Aristocrats based on the S&P 500 is my favorite and the only one that I have studied thoroughly. It is revised annually; therefore, it is always up to date.

I focused a lot on the DA stocks until 2017, at which time I began to notice that some of the stocks continuously lagged the DJIA. Consequently, I began to look for better tools for evaluating stocks, whether DA's or not. There is a plethora of information available on this subject; however, much of it is quite complicated. After much searching, I realized that a new approach was needed, and eventually came up with the stock-picking technique described in Chapter 10.

Dividend Funds–if you are not comfortable picking dividend stocks, you can take a highly diversified approach by investing in funds that focus on dividend stocks. There are numerous exchange-traded funds (ETFs) and mutual funds that focus on dividend income while providing the safety of high diversification.

A succinct analysis of the DJIA is presented in Chapter 8, *The Dow Jones Industrial Average.* By performing this analysis, which covers the last 100-year history of the Dow, I learned to be fairly comfortable with the ups-and-downs of this widely studied index.

Chapter 8
The Dow Jones Industrial Average
(DJIA, Dow 30, Dow)

In 1884 Charles Dow published the first stock prices in a list that would eventually become the DJIA. There were eleven stocks on the list, nine of them railroads; Dow totaled the prices and divided by 11. Originally, he published the results in a newsletter, and, at some time later, in The Wall Street Journal, the oldest continuously published financial index in the world. A few years later, Charles Dow met Edward D. Jones and Charles M. Bergstresser; together, these three men formed Dow, Jones, & Company.

Until 1928, the DJIA was calculated exactly the same as Dow's first calculation; however, at that time it was changed to the weighted index still used today. The weighted index has some advantages, but one major disadvantage is that a large move in a few high-priced stocks can distort the whole index, i.e., the move could send the index one way when the majority of stock prices were actually going the other way.

Since its inception, the Dow Jones Industrial Average has been a widely studied indicator of stock market activity. It is a barometer of the nation's economic health and especially how the health of the economy is viewed through the eyes of investors. It is the most prominent of all stock indexes, with the S&P 500 being the second most prominent.

The DJIA is composed of 30 blue-chip companies, each of which is being analyzed constantly by countless analysts, professional as well as individual investors.

The list of stocks changes from time to time; nevertheless, the DJIA is here to stay. Since it is composed of only 30 stocks, an individual investor can keep up with the performance of each without a Herculean effort. This is not the case with the S&P 500, Nasdaq, or the Russell 2000. The simplicity of the DJIA makes it unique among stock indexes; moreover, the 30 stocks are shored up by heavy institutionalized investment, a fact that helps give them some measure of stability. The current list is shown below.

2021 DOW JONES INDUSTRIALS

3M (MMM)	Johnson & Johnson (JNJ)
American Express (AXP)	JP Morgan Chase (JPM)
Amgen (AMGN)	McDonald's (MCD)
Apple (APPL)	Merck (MRK)
Boeing (BA)	Microsoft (MSFT)
Caterpillar (CAT)	Nike (NIKE)
Chevron (CVX)	Procter & Gamble (PG)
Cisco (CSCO)	Salesforce (CRM)
Coca-Cola (KO)	Travelers (TRV)
Dow (DOW)	UnitedHealth (UNH)
Goldman Sachs (GS)	Verizon (VZ)
Home Depot (HD)	Visa (V)
Honeywell (HON)	Walgreens (WBA)
IBM (IBM)	Walmart (WMT)
Intel (INTC)	Walt Disney (DIS)

I've already stated that *time in the market is more important that timing the market*. To further explore this premise, I have analyzed the growth of the DJIA for the past 100 years by breaking it into 10-year segments and calculating the gain or loss for each decade. The chart is shown below. In addition, I discuss how long it takes for a portfolio to double, something every investor likes to do.

100-YEAR ANALYSIS OF THE DJIA IN TEN-YEAR SEGMENTS

Ten-Year Time Span	Index	Percent Change
1-1-1921 thru 12-31-1930	71.95 - 77.90	8.3%
1-1-1931 thru 12-31-1940	77.90 - 130.57	67.6%
1-1-1941 thru 12-31-1950	130.57 - 239.92	83.7%
1-1-1951 thru 12-31-1960	239.92 - 615.89	156.7%
1-1-1961 thru 12-31-1970	615.89 - 890.20	44.5%
1-1-1971 thru 12-31-1980	890.20 - 963.99	46.8%
1-1-1981 thru 12-31-1990	963.99 - 2633.60	173.2%
1-1-1991 thru 12-31-2000	2633.60 - 10787.99	309.6%
1-1-2001 thru 12-31-2010	10787.99 - 11577.51	7.3%
1-1-2011 thru 12-31-2020	11577.52 - 30606.48	264.4%

*Prices are listed as January 1 to December 31, regardless of the date of first and last trading days each year.

*To avoid having two sets of numbers, the December 31 closing value is also used as the January 1 opening value, although they are seldom identical.

*From:
http://www.fedprimerate.com/prime-rate-website-sitemap.htm

—

Starting on January 1, 1921, at a value of 71.95, the DJIA index doubled 8+ times in 100 years, or one doubling every 12 years on average. According to the Rule of 72 (see note at end of chapter), this equates to 6% capital appreciation compounded annually for 100 years. With the average dividend of the entire DJIA hovering near 2%, the total annualized gain for this 100-year period was approximately 8%.

Most people are not interested in how the stock market did a hundred years ago, so let's examine the last 25 years.

25-Year Time Span   Index Change   Gain

1-1-1996 thru 12-31-2020   5177.45 - 30606.48   491%

With dividends of 2% added to the capital gains, this 25-year period produced total gains of approximately 11% compounded annually. At this rate, an investment will double every 6.5 years.

Now, let's look at the last five years.

5-Year Time Span   Index Change   Gain

1-1-2016 thru 12-31-2020 17405.48 - 30606.48   75.8%

This growth rate is about 12%. With dividends added, the total return for the DJIA was approximately 14% over this 5-year time span.

A growth rate of 14% brings up an interesting proposition. Why not put all of your funds into DIA, the ETF that tracks the DJIA? Seriously, if your portfolio's performance is not approximating the DJIA's growth, then DIA wouldn't be a bad place to put 100% of your cash.

If you can't beat the DJIA, why not join it? Your portfolio would be in sync with an index boasting an upward trend for well over 100 years. We know a lot about the DJIA–enough that we should be comfortable with it over the long haul. It will pull back sharply on an average of once every four years, and the recovery will take a little over one year. Even so, it will continue its climb upward as years roll by.

My prediction: the DJIA will reach 70,000 in six to seven years.

Are you interested in putting all of your funds in DIA?

Well...I'm not interested either, but I'm emphasizing the DJIA's performance to make a point. Every portfolio needs a benchmark. DIA, the fund that tracks the DJIA, is the benchmark by which I measure a stock's performance. It's easy to do, and I'll show you how in Chapter 10.

Let's look at another popular list in Chapter 9, *The Dividend Aristocrats*.

Footnote: I used the Rule of 72 to make the above estimates. The Rule of 72 is a used to estimate the amount of time it takes for an investment to double. The rule is commonly used for calculating dividends but can be used to calculate capital gains or capital gains plus dividends.

The formula is R x T = 72   R = Rate gain (%)
T = Time (years)

This formula gives an estimate, not an absolute value.

Chapter 9
Dividend Aristocrats

The Dividend Aristocrats (DA's) are companies in the S&P 500 that have increased dividends for 25 consecutive years or more. I have studied this list more than any other list except the DJIA. The original list was launched in 2005 and is updated yearly. Companies are added to the list when they reach the 25-year threshold and are removed when they fail to increase their dividend during a calendar year or are removed from the S&P 500. The DA's have been recommended by some advisors as an alternative to bonds for investors looking to generate a steady income stream that does not depend solely on capital appreciation. This list is important, not just to investors, but also to companies on the list. It is not uncommon for a DA having a subpar year to increase their dividend by a tiny amount, just to stay on the list.

About 10 years ago, I started studying the Dividend Aristocrats and concluded that a near-perfect portfolio would consist of all 50+ DA stocks. While this would make a fairly good portfolio, further study indicates that some of the DA's are not good choices because the stocks growth rate is so slow. Examples are Coca-Cola (KO), Johnson & Johnson (JNJ), and Walgreen's (WBA). These stocks will seldom, if ever, outperform the DJIA. If you are a good enough market-timer to buy them near their 52-week lows, they would be good buys, but so would nearly any other stock.

The current list of Dividend Aristocrats is shown below; it was updated in August 2021. Note—the dividends will fluctuate with the price of the stock.

2021 DIVIDEND ARISTOCRATS

Company	Ticker	Dividend, %
3M Company	MMM	3.0
A.O. Smith	AOS	1.5
Abbot Labs	ABT	1.5
Abbvie	ABBV	4.5
Aflac	AFL	2.4
Air Products	APD	2.1
Archer Daniels Midland	ADM	2.5
AT&T	T	7.4
Automatic Data Proc.	ADP	1.8
Becton, Dickinson	BDX	1.3
Brown-Forman	BF.B	1.0
Cardinal Health	CAH	3.3
Caterpillar	CAT	2.2
Chubb	CB	1.8
Chevron	CVX	5.2
Cincinnati Financial	CINF	2.1
Cintas	CTAS	1.0
Clorox	CLX	2.6
Coca-Cola	KO	3.0
Colgate-Palmolive	CL	2.3
Consolidated Edison	ED	4.2
Dover	DOV	1.2
Ecolab	ECL	0.9
Emerson Electric	EMR	2.0
Exxon Mobil	XOM	6.0
Federal Realty Inv. Trust	FRT	3.6
Franklin Resources	BEN	3.8
General Dynamics	GD	2.4
Genuine Parts	GPC	2.6
Hormel	HRL	2.1
Illinois Tool Works	ITW	2.0

Johnson & Johnson	JNJ	2.5
Kimberly-Clark	KMB	3.4
Leggett & Platt	LEG	3.5
Linde	LIN	1.4
Lowe's	LOW	1.7
McCormick	MKC	1.6
McDonald's	MCD	2.1
Nucor	NUE	1.6
People's United Financial	PBCT	4.7
Pentair	PNR	1.1
PepsiCo	PEP	2.8
PPG Industries	PPG	1.4
Procter & Gamble	PG	2.5
Roper	ROP	0.5
S&P Global	SPGI	0.7
Sherwin-Williams	SHW	0.8
Sysco	SYY	2.5
T. Rowe Price	TROW	2.1
Target	TGT	1.4
VF Corp	VFC	2.4
W.W. Grainger	GWW	1.5
Walmart	WMT	1.5
Walgreens	WBA	4.0
IBM	IBM	4.5
NextEra Energy	NEE	2.0
West Pharmaceutical	WST	0.2
Amcor	AMCR	4.1
AtmosEnergy	ATO	2.5
Realty Income	O	4.0
Essex Property Trust	ESS	2.6
Albemarle	ALB	0.8
Expeditors International	EXPD	0.9

Shortly after the Dividend Aristocrat's became popular, ETF's sprang up offering investors the opportunity to own a share of each DA stock by purchasing shares in ETF's that track the aristocrats. Five popular ones are listed below.

ETF's Based on Dividend Stocks

SCHD - Schwab US Dividend Equity
NOBL - ProShares S&P 500 Dividend Aristocrats ETF
SDY - SPDR S&P Dividend ETF
VIG - Vanguard Dividend Appreciation Index Fund ETF
DNL - WisdomTree US Quality Dividend Growth ETF

Note: A SPDR is a specific type of exchange-traded fund (ETF) issued by State Street Global Advisors; SPDR stands for S&P Depository Receipts.

While on the subject of dividends, we may as well cover High-Dividend Stocks.

Note: these stocks are not Dividend Aristocrats.

When people get near retirement age, they often tend to get more conservative. Many invest in CD's, bonds or bond funds, annuities, stocks that pay high dividends, etc. In Chapter 7, I listed four types of high-dividend securities that are popular today. They are repeated below with examples of each type shown in parenthesis.

REIT's: Real estate investment trusts (Examples: NLY, AGNC)
CEF's: Closed end funds (Examples: DDF, SABA)
BDC's: Business development companies (Examples: MAIN, ARCC)
MLP's: Master limited partnerships (Examples: EPD, BIP)

In Chapter 14 we'll compare some of these securities to DIA

First, I'll explain my stock-picking strategy in Chapter 10. It's very simple; you'll wonder why you've never seen it published before.

Chapter 10
The 5/25 Test–a Great Stock-Picking Tool

In one of my science fiction novels, *The Dar Lumbre Chronicles*, cytogeneticists are working with a heart-tissue culture known as DL-666. This culture was named by its inventor, Dar Lumbre, who failed 665 times before getting the desired results on the 666th try. Even though artificial hearts made from DL-666 saved many lives, some religious fanatics found a problem with the number 666.

In real life, I did not fail 524 times before coming up with the 5/25 Test. I use this number to indicate securities that have outperformed the DJIA for 1, 2, 5, and Maximum number of years. Any stock, ETF, or mutual fund that passes the test is designated a 5/25 security. I've assembled three model portfolios of such securities. One is a collection of 10 ETF's, one is a collection of 40 stocks without regard to their size, and the other is composed of 20 small and mid-cap stocks. We will look at the performance of these portfolios in Chapters 11 and 12.

Question: although the 5/25 Test can be used to build a strong portfolio, will critics find a problem with it?

Answer: probably. It doesn't use enough complex charts and graphs to suit most money managers and financial advisors.

Before explaining this stock-picking method, let me give you a short financial autobiography.

1962–Upon graduating from college, I went to work for an oilfield chemical company in Houston. After 12 years, I took a position as a lab manager with another chemical company and worked for them three years before going out on my own.

1977–I left the corporate world early in the year, and, along with my wife, started Johnston Polymer Co., Inc., a company that manufactures a line of polymers which reflect the company name (J-POLY 101A, J-POLY 101C, etc.). We put our life's savings into the company startup. The first year of operation, we opened IRA's at a local bank and funded them for two or three years, pretty much from petty cash.

1980's–Around 1980, we opened IRA accounts with an investment firm and added to them yearly. In the mid 80's, we set up Simplified Employee Pension/Individual Retirement Accounts (SEP/IRA's) for all employees of the company.

By the **late 1980's**, we had accumulated a small amount of savings, and I opened an account with a brokerage firm and bought a couple of mutual funds, both suggested by a financial advisor. While that was a start, it seemed very bland to me. I wanted to buy and sell stocks that I picked out all by myself. I subscribed to *Investor's Business Daily* and *Barron's* and studied both of them diligently. Finally, I got the nerve to pick a stock and instructed my broker to buy it.

What a feeling!

1990's–I started selecting stocks by bottom fishing in the early 90's. It seemed like a good way for a novice investor to start. You know–*Buy low and sell high.* I subscribed to a bottom fishing newsletter; however, relying completely upon someone else's advice was too passive to suit my taste.

About 1995, I discovered Michael O'Higgins' book, *Beating the Dow*, which describes the *Dogs of the Dow* method of picking stocks. I tried the method for a while, although I didn't make the DJIA and the Dogs my entire investment world, as O'Higgins does in his book. The Dogs method worked well, yet I had a problem. My main portfolio is not in an IRA or similarly tax-protected fund; therefore, profit is taxable in the year in which it's earned.

After fumbling around with various methods, I decided that value investing would be the best approach. Starting in the late 1990's, I became a *semi* value investor and did okay in the market for a while. Still, I kept revisiting my stock-picking methods.

2010–I discovered an interesting list of stocks around the middle of 2010, *The Dividend Aristocrats*. I have bought many stocks from this list and continue to hold several of them to this day. I've dissected this DA list many times over the past 10 years. Except the Dow Jones, it is my most-studied list of stocks.

In 2017, I began to realize something was wrong with this list–some of the DA's were not good choices because their stocks grow so slowly. Examples are KO, JNJ, and WBA. These stocks never beat the Dow over an extended period of time, and their dividends aren't large enough to make up for their lack of capital gains (in Chapter 13, I will prove this statement beyond the shadow of a doubt!). I was absolutely determined to find a method to separate the wheat from the chaff.

I pondered this problem for several months in 2017. Then it came to me in a flash–if I wanted to beat the Dow, all I had to do to evaluate a potential stock purchase was to compare it to the DJIA. What could be simpler than that?

Since you can't buy shares in the DJIA as such, I chose DIA as my benchmark. As mentioned before, DIA is an ETF that tracks the Dow. When you buy DIA, you're buying shares in all 30 stocks that make up the DJIA. This makes DIA the perfect benchmark. Moreover, I've come to the conclusion that, if you can't find a stock that can beat DIA, why not buy DIA rather than the stock being evaluated. That seems like a very logical conclusion; moreover, I've recently used it as a *placeholder* a couple of times while trying to pick a stock that might be a better investment.

Early in January 2018, I first used DIA as the benchmark to select a group of 10 ETF's by the 5/25 Test. I bought them all, but have sold two. In Chapter 11, I'll show you how they've performed since January 2018, as well as how they've performed year to date (2021).

In order to perform the simple evaluation described in this chapter, you'll need access to some basic stock market data. You can probably find all you need on your bank or brokerage firm's website. In addition, there is a lot of good information on the internet that is available to everyone. Over the years, I've utilized several websites including cnbc.com, foxbusiness.com, and finance.yahoo.com.

I use Yahoo Finance's website the most; although, at the moment, I'm peeved at them. Here's why: my stock-picking method requires two or three charts to explain it, so I asked Yahoo for permission to use charts from their website; they denied my request, so I had to compose the charts myself.

Note: These three charts have been stylized and generalized, but not *plagiarized.*

Yahoo's website contains a lot of useful information and is simple to use. Since I want you to have ready access to good information, I'm going to refer to them in the following discussion as if they were my best friends.

Before going to the step-wise instructions which follow, study the following run-on sentence for a moment:

Go to Yahoo Finance, pull up a chart for DIA, and compare it to the stock that you're considering at intervals of 1 year, 2 years, 5 years, and Maximum years; if your candidate beats DIA in each of these intervals, put it on your wish list.

That's all there is to the 5/25 Test, yet it works extremely well—so well that I'm surprised that no one has ever touted it as a stock-picking method before. If you ruminate on the above highlighted sentence until you fully understand it, you probably won't need to pay much attention to the rest of this chapter.

Otherwise, here are some more specific instructions:

Go to **https://finance.yahoo.com/** and proceed as follows when the home page appears:

1. Type "DIA" (without quotation marks) in the search box at the top of the page and click on the *Search* icon (the magnifying glass).

A summary page similar to Figure 1 will appear.

2. Click *Full screen* at the right of the small chart shown in Figure 1.

An enlarged chart similar the one in Figure 2 will appear.

Note: the 1-year chart is highlighted; we will also use 2-year, 5-year, and Maximum. I like to use a bar chart for DIA and a line graph for the candidate stock to avoid confusion.

3. Click *Comparison* in the menu above the chart as shown in Figure 2, and a search box will drop down.

4. Type the symbol of your candidate company in the *Comparison* search box. I chose Dover Corporation (DOV) with the chart still set at the 1-year interval, and Figure 3 appeared.

Don't pay too much attention to the numbers along the sides of the graph (I didn't strive for 100% accuracy, anyway). It's not the prices you need to study, it's the concept. All you need to consider is the graph itself, especially how DIA compares to your candidate stock as it slopes upward from left to right. Simple, isn't it?

A Word About the Maximum years?

After some thought, I've slacked off on the stringent "Maximum" requirement. If the candidate stock is good at the first three intervals and fairly close at the Maximum, I put it on my wish list. After all, it seems that any company that has beaten the DOW for 1, 2, and 5 years would be a good prospect. DOV beat DIA at the Maximum years, and scrolling backward through the chart reveals that it has beaten DIA, or, at least, has been competitive to it for more than 20 years.

FIGURE 1. Summary of Information on DIA

(SPDR Dow Jones Industrial Average ETF Trust–DIA) Aug. 31, 2021

Summary Chart News History Profile Financials Analysts

Previous Close	354.57
Open	352.65
Bid	354.91
Ask	354.93
Day's Range	354.78 - 355.07
52 Week Range	261.41 - 356.60
Volume	86,666
Avg. Volume	3,650,125
Net Assets	30.46B
Net Asset Value	350.07
P/E Ratio	3.75
Yield	1.61%
YTD Return	17.18%
Expense Ratio	0.16
Inception Date	1-13-1998

1D 1W 1M YTD 1Y 2Y 5Y Max Full Screen^

355.17

354.95

354.73

354.51

10 AM   12 PM   2 PM

FIGURE 2. One Year Chart on DIA
(SPDR Dow Jones Industrial Average ETF Trust–DIA)

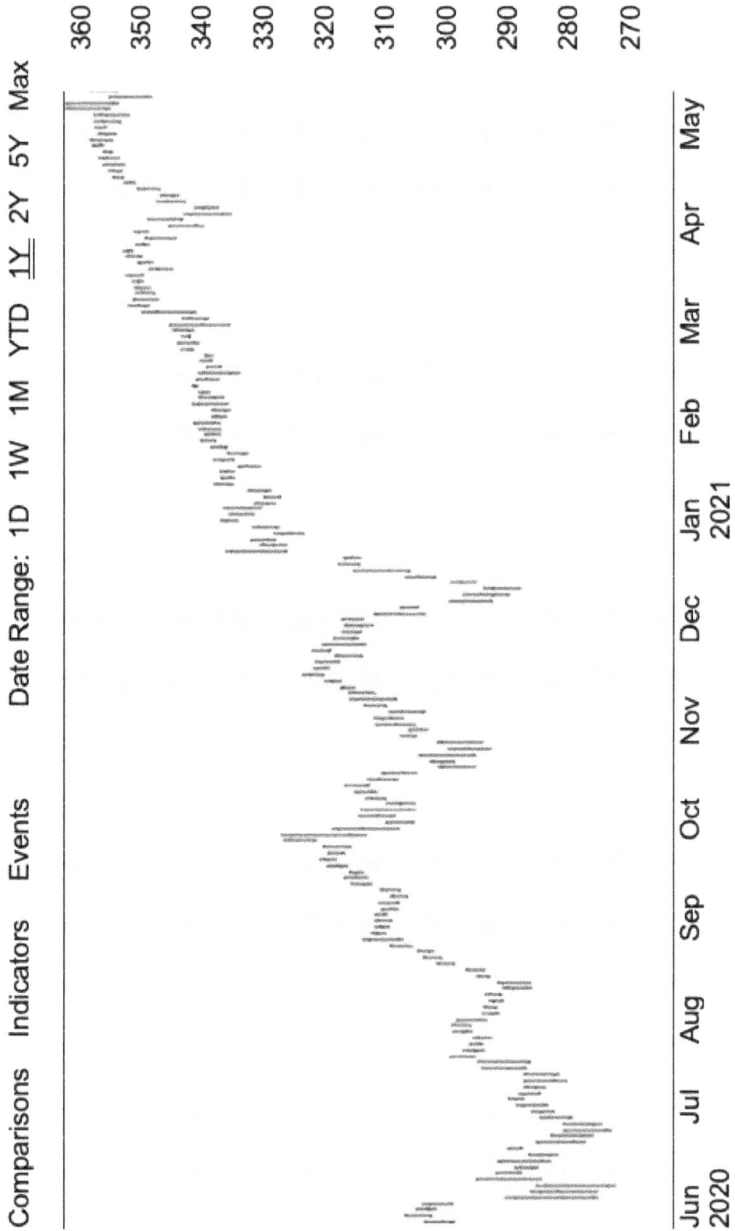

Comparisons   Indicators   Events   Date Range: 1D 1W 1M YTD 1Y 2Y 5Y Max

FIGURE 3. Chart Comparing DOV to DIA at One Year
(DIA represented by bar; DOV represented by line)

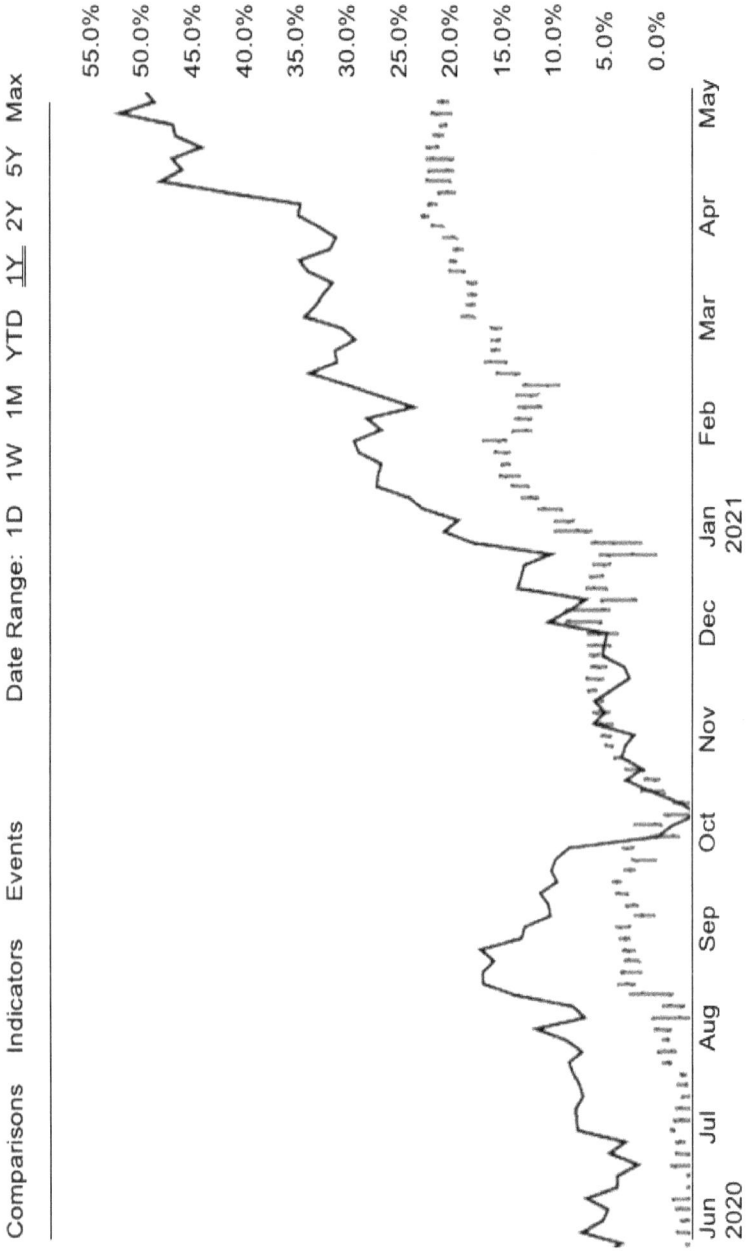

Comparisons   Indicators   Events   Date Range: 1D   1W   1M   YTD   <u>1Y</u>   2Y   5Y   Max

As you can see, DOV outperformed DIA significantly over the one-year interval. This is all there is to the first step of the 5/25 Test. To complete your evaluation, repeat the above test for the remaining time frames. For DOV, the 2-year, 5-year, and Maximum graphs look similar to the 1-year graph, so there's no need to show them. The companies you're evaluating should remain above DIA at each interval; however, I recommend giving them a little slack at the Maximum, as discussed above.

When I put together my list of small and mid-cap stocks, some of them had been in business only about 10 years, so the Maximum was a rather short time period. After some thought, I decided not to put any company on my wish list that had been in business less than 10 years, no matter how badly it had beaten the DJIA.

So, what kind of stock selection method is this?

I see it as a form of momentum investing, except instead of looking for momentum over a short or medium time frame, **this method searches out stocks with perpetual momentum.**

Various finance websites have a lot of other information, but I don't study much of it. However, I definitely look at the company profile to see where it is located, what products and services it offers, how many employees it has, how long it has been in business, and its market cap. I usually check whether analysts think it's a (1) *strong buy*, (2) *buy*, (3) *hold*, (4) *underperform*, or (5) *sell*; however, I seldom let their opinions stop me from buying a stock that passes the 5/25 Test. The only exception is in cases when a large percentage of the analysts rate the stock a *sell*. If that happens, I investigate the company further to see what the problem is. So far, the 5/25 Test hasn't let me down since I started using it over three years ago. Not every stock on my 5/25 wish list has outperformed the DJIA, but the majority of them have done so, many by a wide margin.

In general, I pay very little attention to the company's financials (this statement is going to elicit some criticism, that's for sure!). The reason is this: if the stock has outperformed the DJIA forever, numerous investors have already decided that its financials support the current price.

A stock is worth whatever price investors are willing to pay for it.

Buy some 5/25 stocks and hold them forever. Well...hold them as long as they stay competitive to the DJIA.

Now, let's move on to Chapter 11, and see how my first 5/25 portfolio has performed over the last 3 ½ years.

Chapter 11
Selecting ETF's by the 5/25 Test

In January 2018, I came across a list of ETF's in Kiplinger's magazine and decided to analyze them by my new method, which had yet to be named. Within a couple of days, I assembled a portfolio, largely from Kiplinger's, and bought eight of the ten (all except VB and VBK, both of which I bought later). **My first portfolio selected by utilizing the 5/25 Test is shown below:**

SCHD - Schwab U.S. Dividend Equity ETF
VTI - Vanguard Total Stock Market Index Fund ETF
RYH - Invesco S&P 500 Equal Weight Healthcare ETF
FDN - First Trust Dow Jones Internet Index Fund ETF
VOE - Vanguard Mid-Cap Value Index Fund ETF
VO - Vanguard Mid-cap Index Fund ETF
VOT - Vanguard Mid-Cap Growth Index Fund ETF
VBR - Vanguard Small-Cap Value Index Fund ETF
VB - Vanguard Small-Cap Index Fund ETF
VBK - Vanguard Small-Cap growth Index Fund ETF

The above portfolio includes ETF's based on small, medium, and large-cap companies that fit into the following pattern:

EXCHANGE TRADED FUNDS (ETF's)

	Dividend (Value)	Blend	Growth
Large-Cap:	SCHD	VTI	FDN RYH
Mid-Cap:	VOE	VO	VOT
Small-Cap:	VBR	VB	VBK

As the above chart shows, these ETF's focus either on dividends, growth, or in-between (blend). This is a well-diversified portfolio that covers all bases, and I intend to hold it as long as the performance remains steady.

How did my first venture into 5/25 stock picking work? Well, the proof's in the pudding, and this pudding is tasty.

I evaluated this portfolio as if I'd bought equal dollar amounts of each ETF on the first trading day of January 2018. That isn't exactly how I did it, but it's close. My actual purchases were spread out over a couple of weeks.

From January 2, 2018, until today (August 13, 2021), this portfolio has gained 62.39%. It's outperforming the DJIA (my goal, as you recall), and looks as if it will double in less than five years after inception. That's what I'm talking about!

Let's take a look at how it's currently performing. **From January 4, 2021, until August 13, 2021, this portfolio gained 16.20 %.**

Individual gains of each of the ETF's.

Ticker Symbol	1-2-2018 until 8-13-2021	1-4-2021 until 8-13-2021
SCHD	51.5%	17.9%
VTI	67.1%	20.0%
RYH	71.8%	17.6%
FDN	101.4%	13.2%
VOE	29.2%	21.2%

VO	57.2%	17.4%
VOT	89.1%	13.9%
VBR	30.5%	21.7%
VB	50.6%	14.1%
VBK	75.4%	5.2%

These individual percent gains show a few things worth mentioning, some not so obvious at first glance. Take note of the following:

1. Over the longer time period, growth companies did the best, whether small, medium, or large-cap. These are RYH, FDN, VOT, and VBK.

2. The laggards over the longer time period (VOE and VBR) are performing best in 2021. I've followed these 10 ETF's over the last 3+ years, and all of them tend to grow in spurts, as you would expect. To some degree, that's why I like this well-balanced portfolio. It will be interesting to see how VOE and VBR perform in the coming months; hopefully, they'll catch up.

3. A word about the dividend of these ETF's. I did not add dividends to the gains shown above. VOE (1.2% dividend), VBR (1.6% dividend), and SCHD (2.9% dividend) would have looked better if I had done so, especially SCHD.

Question: Is it best to buy ETF's or stocks?

Answer: It's hard to say. In the next chapter, where we analyze a portfolio of 5/25 stocks, we'll see some that have performed spectacularly, but there is a degree of safety in ETF's since each is made up of many stocks. At any rate, before you buy anything, put it to the test. **There's no need to buy a stock or ETF that lags the Dow.**

Chapter 12
Two 5/25 Stock Portfolios

In December of 2019, after two years of success with the ETF portfolio discussed in Chapter 11, I began to work up a model portfolio of stocks selected by the 5/25 Test. This was not quite the same as the ETF selection. In the case of the ETF's, my aim was to buy them ASAP, which I did. As for the stocks, they were largely a wish list. I already owned fourteen of them, and didn't have the funds to buy any others at the time.

After a fairly quick search, I set up a portfolio (40 stocks) effective the first trading day of 2020. Though it was impossible to predict what any single stock on the list would do, I felt certain the model contained so many good stocks that a portfolio made up of any 10 or more could hardly lose money, and should make a lot.

This portfolio is approaching two years old and was assembled before the COVID-19 pandemic, so it's been *tested by fire*. I plan to redo it this December (2021) but thought you might like to see the original list, so here it is.

My First 5/25 Stock Portfolio

A - Agilent Technologies
AAPL - Apple Computer
ABT - Abbott Laboratories
ADBE - Adobe Incorporated
ALB - Albermarle Corp.
ALGN - Align Technology
AMAT - Applied Materials
AMT - American tower Corp.
AMZN - Amazon Inc.

GRMN - Garmin Limited
HD - The Home Depot
HON - Honeywell Int.
IDXX - Idexx Laboratories
KLAC - KLA Corporation
LDOS - Leidos Holdings
LOW - Lowe's Companies
MA - Mastercard Inc.
MCO - Moody's Corp.

AWK - American Water Works   MSFT - Microsoft
BABA - Alibaba Group   NFLX - Netflix
CDW - CDW Corporation   NVDA - Nvidia Corp.
CHE - Chemed Corporation   PHM - Pulte Homes
CHTR - Charter Com.   PLD - Prologics Inc.
COUP - Coupa Software   PYPL - Paypal
CRM - Salesforce Inc.   ROP - Roper Tech.
DG - Dollar General Corp.   TJX - The TJX Cos.
EXPD - Expeditors Int.   UNH - United Healthcare
FISV - Fiserv Inc.   V - Visa Incorporated
GOOG - Alphabet Inc.   VRTX - Vertex Pharm.

Possible problem alert. When putting together this portfolio, I didn't pay any attention to the size of the companies being added to it. Consequently, I gave Chemed Corporation essentially the same status as Apple Computer. Chemed's market cap (total value of all shares) is 7.2 billion; Apple's is 2.5 trillion. If my quick calculation is right, Apple is about 350 times as big as Chemed, a fact that's probably important to know.

Let's look at how this portfolio has performed from January 2020 until today (August 13, 2021). The gains reported are total gains, not annualized gains. I'm not going to list the performance of each stock individually as I did for the ETF portfolio in the last chapter. The four sentences below tell the story.

1. If I had been terribly unlucky and picked the 10 lowest-performing stocks from the list, my total gain would have been about 3.5 %. That's certainly not what I was hoping for.

2. If I had been lucky, and selected the 10 best-performing stocks from the list, my gain would have been over 85%.

Very nice–but I didn't do nearly that well.

3. Actually, my luck was a little below average. The 14 stocks that I own from this portfolio have produced a gain of about 37%. I'll take that without complaining!

4. Last but not least–the gain for the entire portfolio was well over 50% during the time period discussed (19 months and 13 days).

Note: Dividends are not included in the above calculations; they would have increased the values a small amount.

My conclusion–very few financial advisors are going to beat this portfolio.

After thinking about the above portfolio for a while, I decided to put a similar list together with only small and mid-cap stocks. Here's that story.

The attached small and mid-cap model portfolio was set up on July 23, 2021, using data from the first trading day of 2020. It's just as real as the original; however, it performed so well that many people are likely to think it's a fake, especially since it was assembled *after the fact*. After all, it would take no special skill to search for stocks that have done well over the last few years and claim to have bought them some time ago. However, this is a true story, believe it or not.

To get a list of small and midcap stocks, I looked up the holdings of VB, VBR, VO, VOE, and VBK, the ETF's from my first 5/25 list. These ETF's are composed of small and mid-sized companies. Most of their holdings were much too volatile to pass the 5/25 Test, but I finally found 20 stocks that did. To keep this selection process honest, as well as random, I selected the first 20 stocks that passed the test. They are shown below.

Small and Mid-Cap 5/25 Portfolio

APTV - Aptiv PLC
AVTR - Avantor
BRO - Brown & Brown
CARR - Carrier Global
CMG - Chipolte Mexican Grill
CRL - Charles River Labs.
CTAS - Cintas Corp.
DFS - Discover Financial
DRI - Darden Restaurants
ENTG - Entegris, Inc.

IDXX - Idexx Labs
IEX - Idex Corp.
IQV - Iqvia Holdings
LH - Lab. Corp. of America
MRVL - Marvell Tech. Inc.
PKI - PerkinElmer Inc.
POOL - Pool Corporation
PTC - PTC Inc.
TECH - Go To Technology
URI - United Rentals, Inc.

I always assemble model portfolios by "investing" $10,000 in each stock on the inception date. By doing so, gains or losses can be figured instantly without using a calculator. Of course, you could do the same thing by "investing" $10 in each, but I like the extra zeros! When I got the above model assembled and hit the *return* button to get the total gain, I was absolutely stunned.

The total gain for the portfolio was over 90% from January 2020 until August 13, 2021. Let me emphasize one thing. At the time I set up this model portfolio, I owned only one stock on the list; therefore, at that point, the 90% gain was equivalent to Monopoly money. In an attempt to get a better comparison to the 40-stock portfolio, I selected the five best and the five worst performing stocks for further analysis. Here's that summary:

1. The five lowest-performing stocks gained about 37%.

2. The five best-performing stocks gained over 125%.

3. Not a single one of the stocks lost money.

Question: Could these gains be repeated, or were they a mathematical aberration that is not reproducible?

Answer: Who knows?

I decided to find out.

To get started, I sold everything in my *Casino Account* (even though doing so resulted in a tax liability) and used the proceeds to buy a small position in each of the 20 stocks in the portfolio listed above. I did this the last week of July 2021 and am planning to hold these stocks for at least a year to see if such nice gains will be repeated a second time.

Wish me luck!

Now, in Chapter 13, we'll put the Dow 30 to the 5/25 Test.

Chapter 13
Analysis of the DJIA Stocks

Since DIA is our benchmark, let's evaluate the Dow 30's performance on the 5/25 Test.

As I mentioned earlier, if a stock passes the test at the 1, 2, and 5-year intervals, I give it a pass if the Maximum year chart doesn't run up some kind of red flag. Some stocks that failed to beat the DJIA 20-25 years ago did beat it five years ago, beat it again two-years ago, and did even better at the one-year interval. Such stocks are gaining momentum and certainly merit consideration as possible purchases.

Dow Stocks That Pass the 5/25 Test In Flying Colors

American Express (AXP)	Nike (NIKE)
Apple Computer (APPL)	Salesforce (CRM)
Caterpillar (CAT)	United Health (UNH)
Goldman Sachs (GS)	Microsoft (MSFT)
JP Morgan Chase (JPM)	Honeywell (HON)

These stocks are worthy of consideration by any investor, regardless of his/her investing style.

Though I haven't developed enough data to be sure, I believe the above stocks are better picks than the Dogs of the Dow, also a 10-stock portfolio. One good thing about them is that they are *buy and hold* stocks. There would be no need to sell any of them after a one-year holding period, as a Dogs portfolio would usually require you to do. No tax liability would be incurred on the profit until you sold the stocks, thereby turning your unrealized gains into actual gains.

Dow Stocks That Merit a Second Look

Cisco (CSCO) - lagged a little at the 2-year interval but otherwise okay.

Dow (DOW) - slightly below DIA five years ago, but good at one and two years. Combined with a little bottom fishing, this stock should be okay.

McDonald's (MCD) - doesn't quite pass the 5/25 test, but I like their sausage biscuits too much to sell the stock.

Home Depot (HD) - lagging a little at one year, but a buy and hold stock for me; so is Lowe's although it's not a DJIA stock. Home repair is here to stay.

Visa (V) - very close all the way; I'm keeping it.

Walt Disney (DIS) - close as well.

In summary, about half of the DJIA stocks are worth buying. The rest are questionable. Let's talk about some of the questionable ones.

In Chapter 9, while discussing Dividend Aristocrats, I mentioned that Coke (KO), Johnson & Johnson (JNJ), and Walgreen's (WBA) are laggards. These three stocks are DA's and are in the DJIA as well, so this is a good time to examine them closely. The final numbers will speak for themselves when we compare the stocks to DIA on the basis of growth and dividends earned for a period of five years. In every case, I have rounded off the values to the nearest dollar.

In this analysis, I "invested" $10,000 in each of these stocks on January 4, 2016, and "sold" it on December 31, 2020, at the closing bell. Next, I calculated the dividends on each stock for five years and added that figure to the value of the stock on December 31, 2016. I calculated dividends as follows: $10,000 x percent dividend x 5 years. I didn't compound the dividends because I accumulate them as cash, rather than reinvesting them in the stocks that paid them. For those who reinvest dividends in the *parent* stock, compound dividends are shown in parenthesis next to the dividend figures that are not compounded.

Results for Coca-Cola

Gains from dividends	$ 1,470	($ 1,560)
Gains due to stock appreciation	2,953	
Total gains	4,423	
Total value after 5 years	$ 14,423	

Results for Walgreen's

Gains from dividends	$ 1,940	($ 2,096)
Loss due to decline in stock price	-5,595	
Total loss	-3,655	
Total value after 5 years	$ 6,345	

Results for Johnson & Johnson

Gains from dividends	$ 1,205	($ 1,265)
Gains from stock appreciation.	5,390	
Total Gains	6,395	
Total value after 5 years	$ 16,395	

NOTE: JNJ is surging in 2021, maybe due to their COVID-19 vaccine. Financial advisors are recommending it, and it currently seems to be a good buy, even though its capital appreciation has lagged for a long time. At any rate, it can't pass the 5/25 Test, so it's not a buy for me at this time.

Results for DIA

Gains from dividends	$ 805	($ 832)
Gains from stock appreciation	6,558	
Total gains	7,362	
Total value after 5 years	$ 17,362	

Earlier, I said that I would prove beyond the shadow of a doubt that KO, JNJ, and WBA are not good choices from the Dividend Aristocrat list. The above numbers prove my claim except (possibly) for JNJ. A three-year time frame (or most any other time beyond one year) would show about the same results as this five-year analysis.

Incidentally, Warren Buffett owns a lot of Coca-Cola shares (everybody makes mistakes!). DIA is outperforming KO badly, but since Warren has put nearly half his funds into Apple, he's not too worried.

Let's move on to an analysis of the Dividend Aristocrats in Chapter 14.

Chapter 14
Analysis of Dividend Aristocrats and Other Dividend Securities

By applying the 5/25 Test to the 2021 Dividend Aristocrats, I came up with the following results (all 65 stocks are listed in Chapter 9).

DA's That Pass the Test

Albermarle (ALB)	Nucor (NUE)
Caterpillar (CAT)	Sherwin-William (SHW)
Dover (DOV)	T. Rowe Price (TROW)
Expediters Int. (EXPD)	West Pharm. (WST)

Only eight DA's pass the test without *applying a curve* to the grades. However, the list below shows a group of good companies with a slight miss at one of the time frames, and most of them have performed well over the years.

DA's With a Slight Miss at One, Two, or Five Years
(otherwise okay)

Abbott Labs (ABT)	Illinois Tool Works (IWT)
Archer Daniels Midland (ADM)	Linde Corp. (LIN)
Automatic Data Proc. (ADP)	Pentair (PNR)
Cintas (CTAS)	S&P Global (SPGI)
Emerson Electric (EMR)	W.W. Grainger (GWW)
Pittsburgh Plate Glass (PPG)	

The overall performance of the eleven stocks on the second list is similar to the eight stocks on the first list. Anyone interested in Dividend Aristocrats should consider them.

Some Popular *Also Ran* DA's

Abbvie (ABBV)
Air Products (APD)
Cincinnati Financial (CINF)
McDonald's (MCD)

My suggestion: Concentrate on the above stocks, and don't get lured in by high-dividend stocks like XOM and CHV, which are DA's. These two stocks are not likely to beat DIA over the next 5 years. They certainly didn't show much capital appreciation over the last five. Maybe the above 19 stocks (23 with the *also ran's*) won't beat DIA every year either, but they will probably a give consistent performance as they've done for years.

Comparison of Three High-Dividend DA's With Three Low-Dividend DA's

On a whim, I picked the three highest dividend DA's and compared them to the three lowest dividend DA's over a period of five years.

The results were nearly unbelievable.

The Test Method

The initial "investment" on January 4, 2016, was $10,000 in each stock. Dividend values were taken from Yahoo Finance on August 16, 2021 (these dividend percentages will change as the price of the stock fluctuates). Non-compound dividends were added to the capital gains or losses to get the total value of the investment after five years (in addition, compound dividends are shown in parenthesis). All values are rounded off to the nearest dollar.

Ticker Symbol	Dividend	Price 1-4-2016	Price 12-31-2020
XOM	6.06%	77.19	41.22
CVX	5.26%	89.53	84.45
IBM	4.57%	135.60	125.88
WST	0.15%	59.24	283.31
ROP	0.46%	186.38	431.09
SPGI	0.69%	96.56	328.73

Results for XOM

Gain from dividends	$ 3,035	($ 3,426)
Loss due to decrease in stock price	- 4,662	
Total loss	- 1,627	
Total value after 5 years	$ 8,373	

Results for CHV

Gain from dividends	$ 2,630	($ 2,922)
Loss due to decrease in stock price	-567	
Total gain	2,063	
Total value after 5 years	$ 12,063	

Results for IBM

Gain from dividends	$ 2,285	($ 2,504)
Loss due to decrease in stock price	-716	
Total gain.	1,569	
Total value after 5 years	$ 11,569	

Results for WST

Gain from dividends	$ negligible
Gain due to increase in stock price	<u>37,794</u>
Total gain	37,794
Total value after 5 years	$ 47,794

Results for ROP

Gain from dividends	$ negligible
Gain due to increase in stock price	<u>13,116</u>
Total gain	13,116
Total value after 5 years	$ 23,116

Results for SPGI

Gain from dividends	$ negligible
Gain due to increase in stock price	<u>24,053</u>
Total gain	24,053
Total value after 5 years	$ 34,053

Summary

$30,000 invested in XOM, CHV, and IBM ($10,000 in each stock) on January 4, 2016, would have been worth $32,005 on December 31, 2020. **Profit, $2,005.**

$30,000 invested in WST, ROP, and SPGI ($10,000 in each stock) on January 4, 2016, would have been worth $104,963 on December 31, 2020. **Profit, $74,963.**

Some might think I picked the most unfavorable time-frame possible for the high-dividend stocks. If so, it wasn't deliberate; anyway, it would be difficult (impossible, I think) to find a time-frame of more than a few days in which XOM, CHV, and IBM would look good against WST, ROP, and SPGI.

If high dividends are tempting you, apply the 5/25 Test to the stock in question before buying it, because **a stock is not likely to be competitive without some capital appreciation, regardless of the size of its dividend.**

In Chapter 9, I listed the following ETF's that are based on dividend stocks. These five ETF's do reasonably well on the 5/25 Test and would likely be of interest to the dividend investor.

ETF's based on dividend stocks:

SCHD - Schwab US Dividend Equity
NOBL - ProShares S&P 500 Dividend Aristocrats ETF
SDY - SPDR S&P Dividend ETF
VIG - Vanguard Dividend Appreciation Index Fund ETF
DNL - WisdomTree US Quality dividend Growth

In Chapter 9, I listed the following high-dividend securities. Below, I give them a more complete analysis.

REIT's, CEF's, BDC's, and MLP's

REIT's: Real estate investment trusts.
　　　　Examples: NLY, AGNC

CEF's: Closed end funds. Examples: DDF, SABA

BDC's: Business development companies.
　　　　Examples: MAIN, ARCC

MLP's: Master limited partnerships. Examples: EPD, BIP

None of these securities pass the 5/25 Test for capital appreciation; therefore, they have to stand on dividends alone. I'm going to pick one security of each type and take a close look at it. The ones that dividend-investors seem to talk about the most are NLY, DDF, ARCC, and EPD. Let's put them to a five-year test and compare them to DIA.

Ticker Symbol	Dividend	Price 1-4-2016	Price 12-31-2020
NLY	10.23%	9.32	8.45
DDF	7.37%	8.61	9.16
ARCC	8.08%	14.13	16.70
EPD	8.03%	25.69	19.59
DIA	1.61%	171.05	305.79

Results for NLY

Gain from dividends	$ 5,115	($ 6,274)
Loss due to decrease in security price	-933	
Total gain	4,182	
Total value after 5 years	$ 14,182	

Results for DDF

Gain from dividends	$ 3,685	($ 4,271)
Gain due to increase in security price	638	
Total gain	4,323	
Total value after 5 years	$ 14,323	

Results for ARCC

Gain from dividends	$ 4,040	($ 4,752)
Gain due to increase in security price	1,820	
Total gain	5,860	
Total value after 5 years	$ 15,860	

Results for EPD

Gain from dividends	$ 4,015	($ 4,713)
Loss due to decrease in security price	-2,373	
Total gain	1,642	
Total value after 5 years	$ 11,642	

Results for DIA

Gain from dividends	$ 805	($ 832)
Gain due to increase in security price	7,879	
Total gain	8,684	
Total value after 5 years	$ 18,684	

Since most high-dividend securities do not beat DIA, they cannot outperform 5/25 stocks.

Incidentally, Dollar General (DG) beat all of the high-dividend stocks listed above during the five-year test period.

That's right...*Dollar General!* Have you ever heard of a money manager recommending Dollar General? Neither have I. Maybe they think it's too ordinary. It's not ordinary; take a look at its five-year performance.

Results for DG

Gains from dividends	$ 355	($ 365)
Gains due to increase in security price	19,651	
Total gains	$ 20,006	
Total value after 5 years	$ 30,006	

Dollar General Challenge

I challenge anyone to find a REIT, CEF, BDC, or MLP that has actually beaten Dollar General over the last five years. My email is: **donjohnston716@yahoo.com**. If you track down one, please send the information to me. I'll believe it when I see it.

Stick with dividend stocks and ETF's that pass the 5/25 Test. Then you'll beat the DJIA. Otherwise, you probably won't.

Chapter 15 lists every stock that I own.

Chapter 15
My Portfolios

My two portfolios are shown below; I hope you find them interesting.

Don's *Casino Account* (Also shown in Chapter 12)

Aptiv PLC (APTV)	Idexx Laboratories (IDXX)
Avantor (AVTR)	Idex Corporation (IEX)
Brown & Brown (BRO)	Iqvia Holdings (IQV)
Carrier Global Corp. (CAR).	Lab Corp. of America (LH)
Chipolte Mexican Grill (CMG)	Marvell Tech. Inc. (MRVL)
Charles River Labs (CRL)	PerkinElmer Inc. (PKI)
Cintas Corp. (CTAS)	Pool Corporation (POOL)
Discover Financial (DFS)	PTC Inc. (PTC)
Darden Restaurants (DRI)	Go To Technology (TECH)
Entegris, Inc. (ENTG)	United Rentals, Inc. (URI)

As mentioned previously, my *Casino Account* has been completely overhauled recently. When I developed this list of small and mid-cap stocks that performed so well on the 5/25 Test, I sold everything in the account and bought every stock on the list. Only time will tell if this was a brilliant move or a foolhardy thing to do.

Don's *Best Picks* (Investment Account)

Abbot Labs (ABT)	Honeywell Int. (HON)
Abbvie Inc. (ABBV).	Leggett & Platt Inc. (LEG)
Agilent Tech. Inc. (A)	Lowes Companies Inc. (LOW)
Alphabet Inc. (GOOG)	Mastercard Inc. (MA)
Amazon Inc. (AMZN)	McDonald's Corp. (MCD)
Apple Inc. (APPL)	Microsoft Corp. (MSFT)
Applied Materials (AMAT)	Netflix Inc. (NFLX)

Automatic Data Pr. (ADP)   Nike Inc. (NKE)
CDW Corp. (CDW)   Roper Technologies (ROP)
Dollar General (DG)   TJX Companies Inc. (TJX)
Dover Corp. (DOV)   Cintas Corp. (CTAS)
Emerson Electric Co. (EMR).   KLA Corp. (KLAC)
Garmin Ltd. (GRMN)   Iqvia Holdings Inc. (IQV)
Home Depot Inc. (HD)   Visa Inc. (V)
Laboratory Corp. of America (LH)
Stanley Black & Decker Inc (SWK)
Texas Instruments Inc. (TXN)
Schwab Strategic Dividend ETF (SCHD)
Vanguard Mid-Cap ETF (VO)
Vanguard Mid-Cap Growth ETF (VOT)
Vanguard Mid-Cap Value ETF (VOE)
Vanguard Total Stock ETF (VTI)
Global Lithium & Battery ETF (LIT)

I make all decisions on the above accounts. If something goes awry, there's no one to blame except myself (and that's happened several times). As for my IRA/SEP, I talk with one of the fund managers a couple of times per year; about three years ago, we put most of the funds into the ETF's mentioned earlier, so it takes care of itself rather well.

The above two lists contain a total of 57 stocks. That's about 12-15 stocks above my usual number, but when I got caught up in the 5/25 craze, there was no way to put it into effect except to buy small amounts of several more stocks. I've owned some of these stocks 10+ years and others 5-10 years; however, my *Casino Account* now consists of newly purchased stocks, which means I've "churned" my account far more than usual the last few months. In the future, I'm going to try to limit the annual turnover to 10% or less. After all, I've been preaching *buy and hold*. Now I'm going to try to do it. If you look at *Don's Best Picks* closely, you'll discover a couple of small-cap stocks. I bought them before realizing that it might be best to separate the small and large-cap stocks on the original 5/25 wish list. In my mind, these stocks are in my *Casino Account.*

One other thing about these two portfolios—over half of them are from the ETF's that passed the first 5/25 Test in Chapter 11 and the two 5/25 stock portfolios in Chapter 12. Of these 69 securities (one stock is on both of the lists, otherwise the total would be 70), only three are in the red as of August 25, 2021. A batting average of 66 out of 69 is pretty good. Moreover, there are enough two-baggers and three-baggers on the list to make up for the slackers.

As far as stock-picking goes, that's about it.

Chapter 16 is a collection of miscellaneous ramblings.

Chapter 16
Miscellaneous Ramblings

Since this is the last chapter of *Stock-Picking Revisited*, I have some miscellaneous stories and a bit of information to leave with you.

DJIA vs The S&P 500

Recently, a young friend (a financial advisor) asked why I didn't use the S&P 500 as my benchmark. That was a good question because the S&P 500 is much more broad-based. It has 500 stocks compared to only 30 for the Dow. My answer was that the S&P has so many stocks that I'd never be able to learn much about most of them. On the other hand, the 30 stocks in the Dow are easy to study–the companies and their products are virtually household names.

You could replace DIA with SPY (an ETF that tracks the S&P 500) as the benchmark in the 5/25 Test. Your results would change very little, if any. SPY and DIA track very closely over an extended period of time with SPY slightly outperforming DIA at 1, 2, and 5 years. Either would work just fine.

Taking Year-End Losses

For tax purposes, every year in December I sell stocks that are showing any significant losses. This offsets profits taken during the year. I've even sold stocks with losses in December and bought them again in January. If you do this, wait at least 30 days before repurchasing, or the IRS will call it a *wash sale* and the loss will not be tax deductible. Some people may cringe at the thought of deliberately taking a loss, but if it saves money, why not?

An Old Adage to Ignore

You may have heard *sell in May and go away*. This saying was born when investors began to notice that the first five months of many years are often the best months for the stock market. Starting in June, it seems to get a little erratic. So...should you jump out in May and jump back in later?

"Not hardly, Pilgrim," as John Wayne would say. If your account is not in an IRA or similarly tax-protected account, by selling you turn unrealized gains into profit that is taxable in the year taken. Even if your portfolio is tax-protected, you'd have to be an exceptional *market-timer* to make this approach work better than the *buy and hold* approach.

A Minor Problem With My Portfolios

I have nine Dividend Aristocrats in my portfolio, most of which I've held for a long time and accumulated a nice unrealized gain. Only one (DOV) passes the 5/25 Test with a score of 100%. The other stocks have done well but aren't 5/25 stocks. If it weren't for the tax implications, I would sell them and buy bona fide 5/25 stocks with the proceeds. As it is, that's not practical, so it looks like they'll be in my portfolio for the foreseeable future. Having to keep holding these stocks makes it harder to beat the DJIA, which is something I relish doing as the next section illustrates.

Beating DJIA and Warren Buffett

At the end of each year, not only do I compare my portfolio's performance with the DJIA (as measured by DIA), I also compare it to Warren Buffett's performance as measured by

Berkshire Hathaway (BRK-B). This is quite a contest as the following charts attest.

Don vs DJIA

Year	Winner
2016	Don
2017	DJIA
2018	Don
2019	DJIA
2020	Don

Don vs Warren

Year	Winner
2016	Warren
2017	Warren
2018	Don
2019	Don
2020	Don

So far in 2021, I'm ahead of the DJIA's performance, but Mr. Buffett is a little ahead of me, primarily because he put nearly 50% of his portfolio into Apple–a bold move that I'd be afraid to make.

Going Out On a Limb With Some Bold Predictions

In December of 2020, many questions were being tossed back and forth about how COVID-19 and a new President would affect the stock market. Some people were predicting a market crash in the first quarter and were selling stocks to raise cash. In the midst of this discussion, I wrote the following letter and gave it to a few people.

DON'S STOCK MARKET PREDICTIONS FOR 2021 (FEB. 3, 2021)

1. The market will not have a "correction" during the first quarter (a "correction" is defined as a drop of more than 10%). It may have a "pullback" of less than 10% but no correction.

2. The DJIA will be volatile, but it will reach at least 35,000 by the end of the year.

3. Apple will reach 150 during the second quarter (probably in April).

4. The FANG stocks will outperform any index such as the DJIA, S&P 500, NASDAC, etc. The FANG stocks are Facebook, Apple, Amazon, Netflix, and Google.

5. The FANG stocks plus Paypal and Microsoft (a 7-stock portfolio) will outperform most Financial Advisor's recommendations by a considerable margin.

6. In 2021, my Investment Portfolio (copy available on request) will outperform the DJIA and Warren Buffet (BRK-A and BRK-B).

NOTE: Most Money Managers use "hedge phrases," i.e., might, may, could, or should. Notice that, unlike them, I used "will" (except for the month in which Apple will reach 150).

On Dec. 31, 2021, we will look at these predictions and figure out my batting average.

Back in the first chapter, I said that I could prove a friend bought Apple in 2011 upon my recommendation. Likewise, I can prove that I wrote the above letter early in 2021. Other people have copies.

Let's evaluate the above predictions as of August 18, 2021.

Predictions 1 & 2 have already happened. When a friend asked how I could be so sure the market wouldn't crash in the first quarter, I gave an answer based on politics, rather than the national economy. Since I have friends in both of the major political parties, I'll keep that answer to myself.

Prediction 3 happened in July, rather than in April. Still, that's not too bad. Of course, anyone can predict that Apple is going up, and it will happen sooner or later. The biggest company in the world just keeps on getting bigger.

Predictions 4 & 5–as of today (August 25, 2021), the FANG stocks have gained 21% since the first trading day of 2021 (calculated from a model portfolio with equal amounts invested in each stock).

Are they beating your portfolio?

Prediction 6 is still up in the air. Due to buying so much Apple stock, Mr. Buffett is slightly ahead, but there's still enough time for me to catch him.

As for my portfolios, if you're reading this, you have copies of them.

What About Gold?

Even though we haven't been on the gold standard in a long time, the gold bugs are still alive and well. But is gold really a good investment?

Here are some figures; decide for yourself. Let's go back to 1950, the year I entered high school. On December 31 that year, gold closed at $34.72 per ounce and the DJIA closed at 235.41. Today gold closed at $1792.50, and the DJIA closed at 35,405.50. If you had put $1.00 in gold on the last day of 1950, it would be worth $51.63 today, and one dollar in the DJIA would be worth $150.40.

That's close to 3:1 in favor of the DJIA.

"Gold has soared the last five years," the gold bugs say.

Really?

On August 25, 2016, gold was $1321.50 an ounce, so it has gained 35.6% in five years. On August 25, 2016, the DJIA closed at 18,448.41, so it has gained 91.9% over the same time-span. Nearly 3:1 again. So, gold didn't soar after all, but the DJIA did, and we know how to beat it.

Some gold proponents actually think that one day the country will go to crypto currency backed by gold (yes, I've really heard that!). That's not going to happen. Gold is one of the oldest mediums of exchange, and crypto is the newest. The two don't mix. Crypto backed by gold is an oxymoron. And that's all you need to know about gold.

How About a Dart Board Portfolio?

In 1967, the Forbes Dart Fund was established by throwing 28 darts at the stock listings in the New York Times. This was at the behest of Malcom Forbes, the founder of Forbes Magazine. At mid-year in 1975, Mr. Forbes reported that the portfolio was still beating the experts.

Mathematically, a portfolio of 28 stocks selected randomly by throwing darts would constitute an *average* portfolio. Don't settle for average; the new 5/25 Test explained in Chapter 10 shows you how to develop a portfolio that will outperform the Forbes Dart Fund and most other portfolios as well, no matter what investment method was used to assemble them.

Ripley's Believe It or Not

Unless I give access to my portfolios, there's no easy way to prove all of the claims in this book are true, and it's virtually certain that many people will doubt them. I don't blame the doubters. After all, anyone could look up the prices of stocks five years ago, assemble a model portfolio, and claim to have bought the stocks. Some of the claims may sound a little far-fetched; nevertheless, they're true. Hopefully, my many friends at Sugar Land Baptist Church will believe this story. To a large degree, I wrote this book for them; that's why the e-book is free.

Final Thoughts

You can pick stocks that consistently beat the DJIA by using the 5/25 Test described herein. If you assemble a portfolio of 10 or more stocks by this method, your chances of beating the Dow will be very good. All of the stocks may not beat it every year, but most of them will, and so will your portfolio as a whole.

When the DJIA reaches 70,000 (in six or seven years), you will have doubled your investment!

Wouldn't that be nice?

Happy investing!

THE END

BIBLIOGRAPHY

Books

Although I didn't refer to all of the publications listed below in *Stock-Picking Revisited,* all of them have influenced my thinking.

Logan, Tina, Getting Started in Candlestick Charting, New Jersey, John Wiley & Sons, 2008

Lynch, Peter, with John Rothchild, *One Up on Wall Street,* New York, Simon & Schuster, 1989

Lynch, Peter, with John Rothchild, *Beating the Street,* New York, Simon & Schuster, 1993

Handbook of Dividend Achievers, Moody's, New York, 1992

O'Higgins, Michael B., with John Downes, *Beating the Dow*, New York, Harper Collins, 1990 (also the revised edition in 2000)

Prechter, Robert R., Jr., *The Major Works of R.N. Elliott*, New York, New Classics Library, Inc. 1980

Rogers, Jim, *The Ultimate Road Trip*, New York, Random House, 2003

Stein, Ben, and DeMuth, Phil, *Yes, You Can Still Retire Comfortably*, California, New Beginnings Press, 2005

Zweig, Martin, *Winning on Wall Street*, New York, Warner Books, 1984

Periodicals

Barron's

Kiplinger's Personal finance

Forbes Magazine

The Economist

The Investor's Business Daily

The Wall Street Journal

The New York Times

ABOUT THE AUTHOR

I was born in East Texas a long time ago, and grew up with a sister and a brother. Upon completing high school, I joined the U.S. Air Force and served three years as a jungle survival instructor in Panama. Following my military service, I enrolled in Stephen F. Austin State University and got married. After getting my degree in biology and chemistry, we moved to Houston where our only child, a son, was born.

Upon arriving in Houston, I went to work for an oilfield chemical company. Twelve years later, I took a position as lab manager with another chemical company and worked there for three years before leaving to start Johnston Polymer Co., Inc.

Upon retirement, I became interested in writing science fiction. My first novel, *The Dar Lumbre Chronicles*, was published in 2018 and the second, *The Alamogordo Connection,* in 2020. Another sci-fi novel, *By Means of Peace*, is currently in progress; however, a few months ago, I got writer's block. For some reason, the idea of writing about the stock market became an obsession. Now that *Stock-Picking Revisited* is finished, maybe the science fiction bug will return.

My wife of 53 years died of cancer in 2014, leaving me the patriarch of a small family—a son, a daughter-in-law, three grandchildren, and two great grandchildren. My family is my pride and joy.

I've been a member of Sugar Land Baptist Church for 24 years and have led Bible study classes throughout that time.

www.ingramcontent.com/pod-product-compliance
Lightning Source LLC
Chambersburg PA
CBHW040907210326
41597CB00029B/4998